Tall things

by Annette Smith
Photography by John Pettitt

I look up
at tall things.

3

The giraffes are tall.

The trees are tall
like the giraffes.

A crane is tall, too.

The crane goes
up to the sky.

My skyscraper is tall.

I am tall
like my skyscraper.

My teddy bear
is **not** tall
like me.

My dad is tall.

I come up to here
on my dad.

My mom is tall, too.

I come up to here
on my mom.

One day I will be tall like my mom and dad.